RUTHIE
BOLTON-HOLIFIELD

RUTHIE
BOLTON-HOLIFIELD
SHARPSHOOTING PLAYMAKER

Terri Morgan

Lerner Publications Company • Minneapolis

For my family

The author gives special thanks to Laura Crosser.

This book is available in two editions:
Library binding by Lerner Publications Company
Soft cover by First Avenue Editions
241 First Avenue North
Minneapolis, Minnesota 55401

Website address: www.lernerbooks.com

Library of Congress Cataloging-in-Publication Data

Morgan, Terri.
    Ruthie Bolton-Holifield : sharpshooting playmaker / Terri Morgan.
        p.   cm.
    Includes bibliographical references (p.   ) and index.
    Summary: Profiles the life and achievements of the Sacramento
Monarchs guard, who won a gold medal in the 1996 Olympics as a
member of the United States women's basketball team.
    ISBN 0–8225–3666–8 (hardcover : alk. paper)
    ISBN 0–8225–9827–2 (paperback : alk. paper)
    1. Bolton-Holifield, Ruthie, 1967– —Juvenile literature.
2. Basketball players—United States—Biography—Juvenile
literature. [1. Bolton-Holifield, Ruthie, 1967– 2. Basketball
players. 3. Women—Biography. 4. Afro-Americans—Biography.]
I. Title.
GV884.B656M67   1999
796.323'092—dc21
[B]   98-27822

Manufactured in the United States of America
1 2 3 4 5 6 — JR — 04 03 02 01 00 99

Contents

Ruthie goes up for a sure shot during the gold medal game at the 1996 Olympics.

 *1*

Gold Medal Game

As 32,997 basketball fans began piling into the Georgia Dome, Ruthie Bolton sat in the locker room deep in thought. In less than an hour, the 5-foot, 8-inch guard and her teammates with the U.S. women's Olympic basketball team would face Brazil in the 1996 gold medal game. Ruthie's long wait was nearly over.

Two years earlier, the Brazilian team had defeated the United States in the World Championships held in Sydney, Australia. This year's U.S. team was eager to make up for the loss. Ruthie, one of the last players cut from the 1992 Olympic team, was especially hungry for the gold. Playing in the Olympics and winning a gold medal had been her dream for more than eight years. It was a goal she had shared with her older sister and best friend, Mae Ola.

One year ahead of Ruthie in school, Mae Ola loved basketball and excelled in the sport. The two were still in grade school when Mae Ola inspired Ruthie to begin playing. They were teammates in junior high, high school, and college. After college, Mae Ola played in overseas leagues for two seasons. Even though she had retired from pro basketball, Mae Ola still had wanted to try out for the 1996 Olympic squad. A serious car accident in 1994 ended any chance Mae Ola had of playing in the Olympics, though. From then on, Ruthie decided to achieve the dream for them both.

Despite being closely guarded by a Brazilian player, Ruthie makes a strong move downcourt.

All the players and coaches for the national team were aiming for nothing less than a gold medal.

The road to Atlanta, home of the 1996 Olympics, had been long. Ruthie had made the national team more than a year earlier. Since then, she had been training hard and traveling around the world with the team. There had been 52 **exhibition games** against top women's college and national teams. The U.S. national team won all of those games.

The team also won its first seven games of Olympic competition. A 93–71 victory over Australia, the eventual bronze medal winner, put the United States into the gold medal game. The Brazilian team, also 7–0 during the Olympics, looked tough.

As **tip-off** grew closer, Ruthie took a deep breath and focused on the task ahead. "I was thinking,

'After all those sacrifices, after all that hard work, and all that time away from my family, it's all coming down to this moment,'" Ruthie said later. "It really motivated me."

The U.S. team's loss to Brazil two years earlier was also on Ruthie's mind. "They had beaten us in the 1994 World Championships, and I was determined that there was no way this team would beat us again," she said. "It was time to do or die, and I was determined to win."

Maria Paula da Silva could do little but pass the ball because of Ruthie's tight defense.

Ruthie knew exactly what it would take to defeat Brazil. Head coach Tara VanDerveer and her staff had put together videotapes showing the strengths and weaknesses of the Brazilian team. Ruthie would defend Maria Paula da Silva, Brazil's **point guard** and leading scorer. After watching the videos, Ruthie knew Silva's moves. "Our coaches told me, 'She's Brazil's key player because she controls the tempo of their offense and scores a lot of points,'" Ruthie recalls. "'The key to this game is you stopping her and limiting her scoring.' And that's what I did."

From the start of the game to the finish, Ruthie stuck to Silva like glue. When Silva had the ball, Ruthie stayed between her and the basket to keep her from shooting. When Silva tried to make or receive a pass, Ruthie blocked the passing lanes. She stole the ball five times. When Silva went up for a **rebound,** Ruthie beat her to the boards, finishing with five rebounds to Silva's two.

Ruthie, like the rest of the U.S. team, was also on fire offensively. Brazil had a brief 1–0 lead before Ruthie nailed a 25-foot jumper for three points. After her basket, the United States was never behind. Center Lisa Leslie scored 15 points in the first two periods. Her points led the United States to a 57–46 lead at halftime. With the U.S. squad hitting 72 percent of its shots, only Brazil's 17–13 rebounding edge kept the game close in the first half.

The United States kept dominating in the second half, going on an 8–0 run when play resumed. All 12 of the U.S. players got into the scorebook. Coach VanDerveer began putting in reserves early in the third period. Sheryl Swoopes added 16 points to Leslie's 29. Theresa Edwards also had a strong game, contributing 9 points and 10 **assists.** When the final buzzer sounded, the United States had a convincing 111–87 victory. Moreover, the team had gained many new fans throughout the United States.

While Ruthie scored 15 points and had five assists, her biggest contribution was shutting down Brazil's star player. She held "Magic Paula" to just eight shots and one field goal. "Paula was covered very closely," said Brazil's coach, Miguel Angelo. "She was simply unable to escape."

Minutes after the game, Ruthie was on the awards stand. Ruthie was so ecstatic as the gold medal was draped around her neck that the moment felt unreal. "It was so sweet," Ruthie recalls. "I thought, 'Am I dreaming? And if I am, I don't want to wake up.' Knowing we'd worked extremely hard and sacrificed so much to win the gold, it meant so much to me."

As soon as the ceremony ended, Ruthie found her family. Her father and 11 of her 19 brothers and sisters had attended the game. Ruthie made her way through the crowd to Mae Ola. They hugged, then Ruthie slipped her gold medal around Mae Ola's neck.

When she wasn't creating problems for Brazil on defense, Ruthie found her way to the basket.

"It was always her dream to play in the Olympics," Ruthie said. "To me, she's a much better player than I am. She's much more talented than I am. I felt she should have been here playing in the gold medal game."

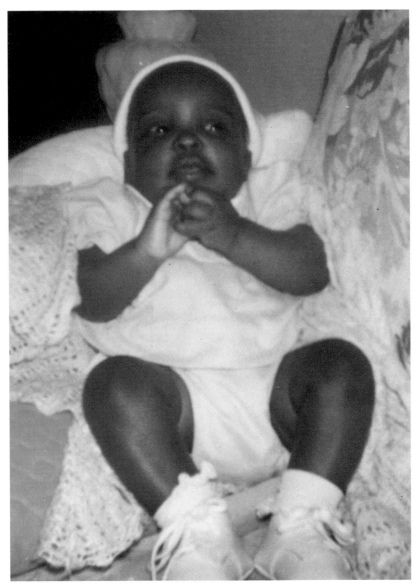

Baby Ruthie

 **2**

Growing Up on "the Flats"

Alice Ruth "Ruthie" Bolton and her twin brother, Ray, were born into a large, loving family in McLain, Mississippi, on May 25, 1967. McLain is a small, rural town of fewer than 900 people. Although the population is small, Ruthie was never lonely. She was one of 20 children born to her parents, the Reverend Linwood and Leola Bolton. Ruthie, the 16th child, grew up surrounded by relatives. The Boltons' extended family—nephews, nieces, aunts, uncles, and cousins—lived nearby and spent much time at the Boltons' five-bedroom house.

"People will say to me, 'That's a mighty large family. How do you find room for all of them?'" said Ruthie's father. "And I'll say, 'If you've got enough love, you've got enough room.'" Linwood Bolton was a Baptist preacher and a farmer. He raised chickens and cows and grew field crops to help feed the family. Leola was busy caring for Ruthie, her 11 sisters and 8 brothers, and tending to a large vegetable garden. "We had a lot of land and plenty of food," recalls Ruthie's sister Mae Ola. "We didn't have to go to the grocery store for anything except sugar and bread."

Ruthie admired and respected her parents, who worked hard to provide for their children. The Bolton family was close-knit, and the children enjoyed spending time together.

Leola, with twins Ray and Ruthie

"We were all close in different ways," Ruthie recalls. "If I had problems in school, I could call on one of my sisters to help out." As in many large families, the older children helped look after their younger brothers and sisters.

Aside from Ray, Ruthie was closest in age to Mae Ola, so the two spent a lot of time together. They loved playing outdoors with their brothers and nephews. The family's home was surrounded by a huge, level yard about the size of six football fields. They called this area "the flats." The Bolton kids used the flats as an athletic complex.

"We played sports pretty much all the time in the fields," Ruthie recalls. "I loved to race in the fields and run in the woods with the boys." Ruthie, who describes herself as "a real tomboy growing up," also loved running relay races and playing football, softball, kickball, and volleyball. Mae Ola also played in the games, and Ruthie tried hard to beat her. No matter what sport they played, however, Mae Ola was always faster, stronger, and more skilled than Ruthie.

From the beginning, Ruthie was very competitive, Mae Ola recalls. Whatever the sport, Ruthie hated to lose. Some days, she'd keep playing until dark, just because she refused to quit without a win.

In those days, Ruthie played mostly against her older brothers James and Paul; her twin, Ray; and her younger brother, Nathaniel. Like Ruthie, the Bolton boys were gifted in sports. Ruthie, however, was determined to hold her own in any type of family contest. "Ruthie had to work hard to keep up with the boys," Mae Ola said. "Her focus and determination all started at home."

Ruthie remembers her childhood home fondly. "It was like a summer camp, with a lot of different activity stations," Ruthie said. "There [were] always a lot of exciting games going on. I really enjoyed those years."

So did many of Ruthie's cousins, nephews, and nieces. "They'd rather stay on the floor at our house—rather than go home and sleep in their own beds—so they could spend more time playing," Ruthie said. Sometimes Ruthie found herself sharing her room with seven other girls.

It wasn't all just fun and games at the Bolton house, though. Ruthie, like her brothers and sisters, had to wash dishes, clean the house, do laundry, and help her mother with a large vegetable garden. With so many people in the house, each child needed to pitch in and help with chores.

"We had to clean house and do fieldwork even before we did our homework," Ruthie said. From these early duties, Ruthie learned to budget her time. She found that if she started right in on her chores and worked hard at them, she would still have time to play.

Along with a love of sports, the Boltons also shared a love of music. All the children played instruments.

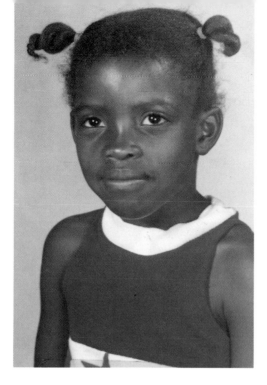

As a young girl, Ruthie was very active.

Except for Ruthie—she could never sit still long enough to practice. Often, they would gather around the family piano, with one of the boys playing, and sing together. They sang mostly gospel tunes, their favorites. Linwood, who preached at five churches, brought his children with him to join the choir. "Back then, singing wasn't a hobby for me like it is now. It was a duty," Ruthie said.

When Mae Ola started junior high school and joined the basketball team, Ruthie looked forward to the following year when she could try out for the squad. When the time came, her years of running races and playing sports paid off. Ruthie made the team easily as a seventh grader. The following year, she was one of the team's top players. When her eighth-grade season ended, Ruthie was invited to join the high school team. Its season was just beginning.

Despite her early success, Ruthie didn't realize how good she was, partly because Mae Ola was even better. Mae Ola led the McLain girls' basketball team to the state championship three years in a row. She was one of the top high school girls' basketball players in the country, and she won numerous awards—including a berth on the All-America team.

All through Mae Ola's prep career, coaches, sports fans, family, and friends all raved about her athletic skills. Everyone assumed she would star in college and play pro basketball overseas.

While Mae Ola received a lot of attention, Ruthie was often overlooked. She played mostly for fun until her sophomore year. Then college coaches began recruiting Mae Ola, who was a junior, for their teams. Ruthie started thinking about playing in college and began working harder at improving her skills.

Some of Ruthie's greatest thrills on the court came during the 1983 and 1984 state high school championships. During her sophomore season, the McLain Rams trailed the team from Houlka by one point with just seven seconds left in overtime. McLain **inbounded** the ball on its end of the court and passed it to Mae Ola, who was near the free-throw area. Mae Ola spun, put the ball up, and watched it hit the rim. It rolled around the hoop several times before finally dropping through the net to give McLain the state title.

The following year, McLain faced Houlka again in the state finals. "That time, there was a lot of pressure on us, because we had beaten them the year before and they were hungry," Ruthie says. With a minute left in regulation, McLain trailed by six points. Mae Ola had fouled out with five minutes remaining.

"We started to give up," Ruthie said. "But our coach called a timeout, and told us to look at the trophy. We did, and he told us it could be ours if we really wanted it."

Inspired, McLain fought back to within one point. With just seconds remaining in the game, McLain passed the ball inbounds. Ruthie was at the top of the **key,** in almost the same spot Mae Ola had been the year before. This time, however, Ruthie was surrounded by defenders. "My cousin was wide open under the basket, so I passed it to her, and she made a **layup** and won the game for us," Ruthie recalls. "We were ecstatic, but the other team was so devastated by the loss, they were crying."

McLain returned to the state tournament the following year, when Ruthie was a senior. Playing without Mae Ola, who had graduated the previous spring, the Rams lost in the second round, ending their two-year streak as state champions.

Ruthie developed into a fine point guard for the Auburn
University Lady Tigers in the late 1980s.

 **3**

Auburn University

Ruthie began planning for her future when she was a high school senior. She knew college could help her get ready for a good career. Ruthie also thought about teaming up with her sister again. Mae Ola had begun her first year at Auburn University in Auburn, Alabama, and was making a huge impact on the school's basketball team.

Auburn was about 180 miles from McLain, close enough for regular trips home. Ruthie liked Auburn for another reason. As a member of the Southeastern Conference (SEC), Auburn's sports teams play against some of the toughest teams in Division I—the highest level of college sports. Ruthie had worked hard to improve her basketball skills in high school. In college, she wanted to test herself against the top teams.

First, she had to convince Joe Ciampi, the head coach, to let her play for him. Ciampi knew that

Ruthie, who had been named to Mississippi's all-state girls' basketball team as a senior, was capable of playing college ball. He thought, however, that Ruthie would find it tough to follow in Mae Ola's footsteps at Auburn. Undaunted by her sister's successes on the court, Ruthie talked Ciampi into giving her a chance.

"She adamantly told me and the coaching staff that she wanted to come to Auburn," Ciampi said. "She said all she wanted was to be given an opportunity to show us what she could do."

Ruthie convinced Ciampi that Auburn was the right place for her and received a full **scholarship.** Even so, she worried about money. The scholarship wouldn't cover all of her living expenses. To help make up the difference, Ruthie joined the Army Reserves.

Auburn coach Joe Ciampi wondered if Ruthie should be on the same team as Mae Ola.

By the time Ruthie joined the team, Mae Ola had already made her mark on Auburn basketball.

Joining the Army Reserves was a major commitment. Ruthie would have to participate in the Army Reserve Officers Training Corps (ROTC) program during her four years at Auburn. Then, after she graduated, she would serve at least two weeks each year in the Reserves for another 11 years.

When school began, Ruthie was very busy. Every morning, she would get out of bed at dawn and dress in her Army clothes and combat boots. Her ROTC unit met at 5:30 A.M. to perform drills and run two miles. Afterward, Ruthie would change into regular clothes and head to her classes. She devoted her afternoons to basketball practice and her evenings to studying.

Coming from a small high school, Ruthie worried about her grades in college. "I was a fair student coming out of high school, but I was nervous about how I'd do in college because McLain didn't have a strong academic program," Ruthie said. The challenge made her work hard. Ruthie approached her studies with the same determination she showed on the basketball court.

In her little free time, Ruthie would join Mae Ola at a local church, where they sang in the choir. Whenever possible, once or twice a month, the sisters returned home to McLain for the weekend.

Worried that Ciampi would make her choose between ROTC and basketball, Ruthie didn't tell him about her military training. Eventually, though, Ruthie's coaches discovered how she was spending her early morning hours. "We started seeing a strain that wasn't like Ruthie," Ciampi told The Associated Press. "But she kept it a secret for the longest time."

Instead of being angry, Ciampi was proud of Ruthie for working so hard. "Here was a young lady playing 34 minutes a game, practicing all out, and also doing her military training," Ciampi said. "As we talked and found out what she was doing, we started to trim down some of her physical activity.

"You're never going to stop Ruthie," he added. "We just tried to slow her down a little."

Ruthie got into 30 games her freshman year, playing mainly as the backup point guard behind junior Helene Barody. When Ruthie was in the game, she handled the ball, driving downcourt to set up the offense. She also concentrated on defense. Crashing the boards fiercely, she averaged 4.8 rebounds per game. She snared 47 steals during the season. Although Ruthie wasn't playing an offensive role, she still managed to score 9.9 points per game, shooting 53 percent from the field. She started 6 of the 30 games she played and had 41 assists.

Auburn finished the season with a 23–4 record and an invitation to play in the NCAA tournament. Mae Ola was the Lady Tigers' highest scorer with 13 points as Auburn downed Southern Illinois in the first round. A few days later, Ruthie matched that total in a heartbreaking 56–55 overtime loss to Mississippi.

During Ruthie's sophomore season, 1986–1987, Barody was a senior and still Auburn's starting point guard. Ruthie came in off the bench in every game and averaged 2.9 rebounds and 8.3 points per contest. The Lady Tigers posted a 26–1 record for the regular season. Only a 72–71 loss to Georgia prevented Auburn from going undefeated. Auburn got revenge during the finals of the conference tournament. There, Auburn trounced Georgia, 83–57, for the SEC title.

As a junior, Ruthie played a key role for the highly ranked Lady Tigers.

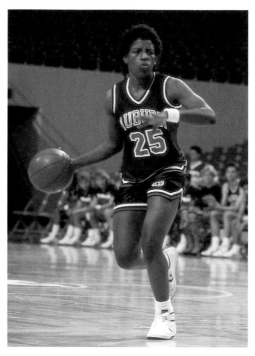

Returning to the NCAA tournament, the Lady Tigers advanced to the third round with wins over Illinois and Old Dominion. A 77–61 loss to Tennessee ended their season. Ruthie's steady play during her first two years of college erased any doubts Ciampi had about her before she entered Auburn. "Ruthie Bolton is what all good things in college basketball are about," Ciampi told reporters. "She worked to excel in the classroom, on the court, and as a person. She led by her actions and was a very important part of our success here."

In her junior year, Ruthie was even more active in Auburn's offense as the starting point guard. She averaged 9.6 points a game. On the defensive end, she snared 108 rebounds and stole the ball 69 times. Undefeated in conference play, the Lady Tigers were 32–3 overall during the 1987–1988 season. Returning to the NCAA tournament for the third straight season, Ruthie helped lead the Lady Tigers to the finals against Louisiana Tech. Auburn lost, though, 88–81.

Ruthie's success continued into her senior season.

Ruthie led Auburn to its third consecutive SEC title in the 1988–1989 season. Playing steadily on both ends of the court, she snared 143 rebounds and shot 37.5 percent from **three-point range.** She led the team with 195 assists. Ruthie capped her senior year with a second trip to the NCAA finals. But again the national title eluded her.

Auburn's 76–60 loss to Tennessee haunted Ruthie for years. Despite having a hot shooting hand that day, Ruthie stuck to her playmaker role, feeding her teammates rather than trying to score. "I've always been a team player, so I kept passing the ball and trying to set up my teammates," Ruthie recalls. "Now that I'm a more mature player, I'm prepared to make better decisions. I know now that if I'm in a game and I'm hot, I need to shoot more."

Ruthie didn't have much time to dwell on the loss. When the tournament ended, she began preparing for final exams. After the last test, Ruthie decided to celebrate by going out for a snack. She stopped at a gas station first, where a deputy sheriff named Mark Holifield noticed her and introduced himself.

"He recognized me from the basketball team," Ruthie recalls. "It was just after our loss in the NCAA finals and we started talking about it."

The conversation went well, and the two hit it off. They began dating often. Since Mark likes to stay in shape too, he and Ruthie began running and working out together. Soon, they were spending all their free time with each other.

In June 1989, Ruthie graduated from Auburn with a degree in exercise physiology, which qualified her to work in sports, perhaps as a coach or trainer. During Ruthie's four years at Auburn, the Lady Tigers had compiled a 119–13 record. They won three SEC titles, made four trips to the NCAA tournament, and competed in the semifinals twice. Ruthie also tallied numerous honors for her play, including being named to the 1988 Final Four All-Tournament Team. Ruthie finished her college career with 526 assists—second in the history of the school—and 246 steals.

Of all her accomplishments in college, Ruthie is proudest of the recognition she received for combining academic and athletic excellence. Her classroom grades, combined with her skill on the basketball court, netted Ruthie spots on the SEC all-academic team rosters in 1988 and 1989.

Playing for USA Basketball's international teams helped Ruthie prepare for an overseas career.

4

Launching a Pro Career

The route to U.S. Olympic basketball teams runs through USA Basketball. The organization, based in Colorado, picks and sponsors the various teams that play for the United States in international tournaments. For example, U.S. select teams are made up of young college students who may one day be Olympic-caliber players. Older college students and recent graduates play on other teams that compete every two years in the World University Games.

USA Basketball also sends squads to compete in the World Championships, held every four years midway between Olympic years. Countries must qualify through regional tournaments, and USA Basketball also picks the teams that will play those games. Another major international tournament is part of the Goodwill Games, held every four years since 1986. USA Basketball holds tryouts for each of the U.S.

teams prior to the tournaments. The players who make the cut come together to play in the competitions, then return to their high school, college, or pro teams afterward.

Ruthie was in fantastic shape and at the top of her game when she graduated from Auburn. Eager to continue playing competitive basketball, Ruthie tried out for the 1989 U.S. select team. Both Ruthie and Mae Ola made the team and traveled to Europe with the squad in the fall. For two weeks, they toured Italy and Czechoslovakia, playing against the top female basketball players in those countries. "It was a good experience," Ruthie said. "It was exciting to travel overseas. We had a good team and did well, although we didn't face any major competition."

The U.S. team played 10 games in Europe and won them all. More important for Ruthie, the trip gave her an opportunity to play on the international level for the first time. International basketball rules and regulations differ from those used by college and pro teams in the United States. For instance, international courts are shorter and narrower, the **free-throw lane** is much wider, the distance for three-point shots is longer, and the ball is larger. Ruthie thought she played well, despite the changes. "I made the transition [from collegiate to international competition] easily," she recalls.

After returning from Europe, Ruthie began getting

ready for a professional career. At that time, the only way for women to earn money playing basketball was to go overseas. Mae Ola had signed with a women's team in Italy after graduating from Auburn in 1988. Following her older sister overseas would allow Ruthie to make a living doing what she loved. It would also help her keep her game sharp. Ruthie had already decided to try out for the 1992 U.S. Olympic women's team.

Ruthie had spoken with an agent while still in college. After she graduated, he landed her a contract to play for a team in Sweden. When Ruthie signed for the 1990–1991 season, she became the first American woman on the roster of a professional Swedish basketball team. In the meantime, Ruthie's relationship with Mark had grown. They had decided to get married.

Ruthie and Mark, around the time of their wedding

In September, before Ruthie was supposed to leave for Sweden, she and Mark went to the local courthouse. There, before a justice of the peace, they married. After the wedding, Ruthie had to decide what name to use. She had established a basketball career under her maiden name of Bolton. She was also very proud to be married to Mark. Initially, Ruthie decided to keep using her maiden name professionally, and a combination of both names for her private life. After a while, she began to use Bolton-Holifield professionally, as well as in her personal life.

After a brief honeymoon, Ruthie flew to Europe while Mark stayed in Auburn. Playing overseas was a huge challenge. "It's really hard being that far away from home," Ruthie said. "The biggest sacrifice is not seeing your friends and family."

Ruthie also disliked being the only American on her team. The team hired a translator to help her talk to coaches, teammates, and the media. The translator would listen to what Ruthie said in English, then repeat it in Swedish. Likewise, the translator would listen to what others said in Swedish and repeat it to Ruthie in English. Still, Ruthie found it frustrating not to be able to talk directly with people. She also missed Mark. In Sweden, she found herself going home to an empty apartment after practices and games. Ruthie was used to having a lot of people around.

"It was a new lifestyle, a whole new way of living,"

Ruthie said. "I coped by making new friends and trying to make the best out of it. . . . I called home a lot, especially to Mark," Ruthie said.

Ruthie also faced other challenges. Since basketball was invented in the United States, many people expect U.S. players to be the best in the world. In the European leagues, U.S. players generally receive star billing. With that honor, however, comes responsibility. "As an American player, you get the fame and the blame," explained Mae Ola, who was playing in Spain while her sister was competing in Sweden. "You're under a lot of pressure to carry the team."

Ruthie's team qualified for the playoffs and finished second in the postseason championships. After the games were over, Ruthie flew home to be with Mark. She also couldn't wait to visit her family in McLain. Many of her older brothers and sisters had married and were raising families nearby. The visits home gave Ruthie a chance to catch up with her family and relax. During the day, there usually was a pickup basketball game going on at the family's court. In the evening, the Boltons would gather around the piano and sing their favorite gospel songs—just as they had when Ruthie was growing up.

But Ruthie didn't have much time to visit. First she had to fulfill her yearly commitment with the Army Reserves. After serving two weeks of military duty, Ruthie joined the U.S. team that played in the World

Universities Games. Ruthie led the team in scoring, averaging 14 points per game. She also averaged 4.5 rebounds and led the United States to a gold medal. For her outstanding play, Ruthie was named the 1991 USA Basketball Female Athlete of the Year.

In between seasons for her overseas teams, Ruthie represented the United States in international games.

In the fall, Ruthie began preparing to return to Europe for the 1991–1992 season. She had signed with a team, Tungstrum, in Hungary. Again, Ruthie would be the first U.S. woman to play professionally in that country. The season went well. Tungstrum had a winning season, finishing second in the league. Ruthie was happy with her game and less lonely than the year before. Mark had put his career as a deputy on hold to accompany Ruthie in Europe. Ruthie appreciated Mark's sacrifices for her career. "He's a really big fan of mine," she said. "He's been right there with me through the thick and the thin all these years."

When the playoffs in Hungary ended, Ruthie and Mark returned to the United States so Ruthie could prepare for another national team tryout. USA Basketball was assembling a women's team to compete in the 1992 Olympic Games. Eventually, Ruthie was one of 18 finalists competing for 12 spots on the team, but she missed the cut. "It was disappointing," Ruthie said. "[But] anytime you go for something that elite, the level of competition is going to be high."

Although Ruthie missed the cut for the 1992 Olympics, she earned a gold medal in the 1994 Goodwill Games.

Rebounding from Disappointment

Ruthie sat down to re-evaluate her goals after being cut from the 1992 Olympic team. She would have to wait four more years before she could try out for another Olympic squad. Ruthie knew that pro athletes have relatively short playing careers. Mae Ola had retired from professional basketball in 1991 after playing just two seasons in Europe. Tired of the challenges and loneliness of competing overseas, Mae Ola had returned to the United States to begin a teaching career. "At the time, I didn't know if I'd play [professionally] four more years," Ruthie said. "I knew I wanted to play more basketball though."

Originally, it had been Mae Ola's dream to play in the Olympics. She had tried out for the team in 1988, but wasn't selected. Since Mae Ola had retired from basketball, making the team had become even more important to Ruthie. Eventually, Ruthie decided to try again in 1996. That meant staying in top shape for four more years. Her first step was to prepare for another season in Europe.

Working even harder than she had in the past, Ruthie began preparing for her third pro team. She would join the C.A. Faenzia team in Italy. The Italian league was the world's top women's league. The games would be tougher, and Ruthie was eager to prove she belonged.

Ruthie felt at ease when she and Mark arrived in Italy. As a third-year veteran, she had become more comfortable living and playing in Europe. Also, in Italy, Ruthie was no longer the first U.S. woman to play in the league. A number of other women from the United States, including Mae Ola, had preceded her. Many of her coaches and teammates spoke English, which made communicating easier. "It was really nice coming to Italy," Ruthie said. "I adjusted quickly. They are more accustomed to Americans."

When the season started, Ruthie had little trouble with the higher level of play. She coordinated the offense and became more of a scoring threat than she had been in college—or even in Sweden and Hungary. Rather than automatically looking for an assist, Ruthie began looking for the open shot. She quickly developed into one of the team's top scorers, averaging 26 points per game. The team won more games than it lost but failed to qualify for postseason play.

Off the court, Ruthie and Mark went sightseeing and visited the new friends they had made. Ruthie also called home regularly, keeping in touch with her parents, sisters, and brothers.

When the 1992–1993 season ended, Ruthie and Mark returned to the United States. Ruthie tried out for and was named to the U.S. national team that would compete in the summer. Since the Olympics had been held the previous summer and the World Championships were set for the following year, 1993 was an off year for major international competition. Ruthie and her teammates would be playing to earn the United States a berth in the 1994 World Championships. Ruthie averaged 14.3 points per game, second best on the team, as the American women won the event and a slot in the 1994 tournament.

Ruthie's scoring role increased when she returned to Italy with a new team, Erreti Faenza, for the 1993–1994 season. She averaged 28 points per game. That season, Ruthie became even more active on the boards, hauling down an average of 7.1 rebounds per game. Despite its winning record, Erreti Faenza failed to qualify for the playoffs.

Off the court, Ruthie had grown even more comfortable with Italy. She had begun learning bits of the Italian language the previous year. During her second season, she could talk with her teammates in Italian. In addition to singing her favorite gospel songs, Ruthie sang in Italian as well. She even began singing Italian opera songs after attending several opera performances.

Back in the United States during the summer of 1994, Ruthie was busier than ever. After living in Auburn for years, she and Mark had decided to move to Gainesville, Florida. They would live in an apartment there whenever they were in the country. Mark would also start his high school teaching and coaching career there. Ruthie and Mark had barely settled in, however, when Ruthie needed to go overseas again.

Ruthie races downcourt with the ball during a Goodwill Games matchup.

As a member of USA Basketball's World Championship team, Ruthie flew with her teammates to Sydney, Australia, for the tournament. Setting its sights high, the U.S. team was aiming to win a gold medal. The squad won its early games, then met Brazil in the semifinals. The Brazilian players were playing especially well, and they were even more eager to win. Brazil upset the U.S. squad, 110–107, forcing Ruthie and her teammates to settle for a bronze medal. Then they later watched the Brazilians celebrate their gold medals.

Ruthie didn't have much time to dwell on the team's third-place finish. The 1994 Goodwill Games were also held that summer in St. Petersburg, Russia. Ruthie, who had averaged just 9.3 points per game in Sydney, boosted her scoring average to 11.8 points in the Goodwill Games. Hauling down six rebounds and tallying one and a half assists per game, Ruthie also shot .526 percent from three-point range. Team USA was playing especially well, winning every one of its games en route to a gold medal.

Ruthie returned to Italy in the fall of 1994 for her second season with Erreti Faenza and her third season in Italy. Shortly after she returned, members of a band called Antidum Tarantula invited her to join them. Ruthie accepted, and began performing as the group's lead singer between games. "Although the band played mostly Italian music, we did perform a few American songs," Ruthie said. "It was a lot of fun."

The Boltons fill a house at Christmastime.

Joining the band helped ease Ruthie's homesickness, but she still looked forward to going home. At Christmas time, Ruthie and Mark flew to Mississippi to spend the holidays with Ruthie's family. Normally, Christmas was a joyful time for the Boltons, but in 1994 the holiday was bittersweet. Ruthie's mother, Leola, had developed cancer and was very sick. Ruthie and her brothers and sisters realized it was the last Christmas they would celebrate with their mother. When Leola died a month later, Ruthie was deeply saddened. Playing basketball helped her keep her mind off her loss.

Focusing more on distributing the ball than she had in previous years, Ruthie saw her scoring average dip slightly. She averaged 25.5 points and six rebounds per game during the 1994–1995 season. Her unselfish play paid off. The team improved its won–lost record over the previous two seasons and made the playoffs. They were eliminated in the first round, however.

Overall, Ruthie says, she enjoyed her years in Italy very much. "The competition is good, and the food is good too," she said.

Little did Ruthie know in 1995 that she would soon have pro basketball opportunities in the United States.

6

A Gold Medal and Beyond

Ruthie concentrated on a single goal when she returned to the United States from Italy in the spring of 1995. USA Basketball was assembling the core of its 1996 Olympic team more than a year ahead of the opening ceremonies. Ruthie was determined to make the team this time around.

USA Basketball was equally determined that the United States win gold in women's basketball at Atlanta. Embarrassing losses in the 1992 Olympics and the 1994 World Championships had prompted USA Basketball to assemble the team early. This national team would prepare for the Olympics by playing against college teams and other countries' national teams. In exchange for a salary of $50,000, the players on the team would devote a year to USA Basketball. For some players, that amount was far less than they could have earned overseas.

Ruthie quickly became a steadying influence on her new teammates.

Like Ruthie, Mae Ola wanted to make the 1996 team. In 1994, three years after retiring from the pro game, Mae Ola began working out on the court again. Unfortunately, her Olympic hopes were shattered in a serious car accident. Although she would recover from her injuries, the wreck ended Mae Ola's comeback. Afterward, Ruthie became even more determined to represent the Bolton family on the Olympic team and help Mae Ola share the dream.

After the tryouts, Ruthie and her family were ecstatic when she was named to the team. The squad began training—and traveling—together in the fall. The first leg of exhibition games would have them playing against the top college basketball teams in the United States.

Ruthie and her new teammates put their lives on hold to prepare for the following year's Summer Olympics. "Very little goes on outside of playing basketball right now," said center Lisa Leslie after the team began training together. "You give up your life when you choose to be with a team for a year."

The exhibitions began at the University of Georgia on November 2, 1995. Sheryl Swoopes scored 27 points to lead the national team to a 100–53 victory over one of the top women's college teams in the country. Over the next three months, the Olympians dominated their competition, winning all 20 games against collegiate squads by an average of 46 points. They finished the NCAA tour with a 98–61 win over Texas Tech on February 3, 1996.

Ruthie started 17 of the 20 games on the NCAA tour and averaged 12.6 points and 2.8 rebounds per game. Shooting 52 percent from two-point range, Ruthie also nailed 26 of her 75 three-point attempts. She finished the college tour with 40 assists and 37 steals.

Ruthie's leadership and work ethic impressed her teammates and coaches. Her fellow players saw how hard Ruthie worked during practices and were also motivated to work harder. "Ruthie Bolton is an incredible, special athlete and person," said Coach VanDerveer. "She's the type of player you want to go to battle with. She's so mentally tough, and that's something she gives us that's so important.

"Ruthie exemplifies everything good about an athlete and a competitor," VanDerveer added. "Very few coaches have players [who] inspire them, and she inspires me."

In addition to tuning up for the Olympics, the team used the tour to promote women's basketball. At each stop, the national team held open workouts so fans could watch them practice. They also put on youth basketball clinics at local schools and clubs. Ruthie and her teammates gave motivational speeches to groups in every city they visited.

National team coach Tara VanDerveer thought highly of Ruthie's skills.

While the team's schedule kept her very busy, Ruthie also found time to have fun. She often entertained her teammates by singing during practices. She and forward Nikki McCray worked out a duet of "The Star-Spangled Banner." The two performed the national anthem together well enough to sing it before several of their exhibition games. Ruthie's family also got into the act when the national team traveled to Ruthie's college, Auburn, for an exhibition contest in January 1996. They sang for the audience before the game and at halftime.

After going undefeated against the nation's top college teams, the U.S. squad began a series of international exhibitions. They flew to Russia for seven games against pro teams. The national team won all of its games, and Ruthie was the top scorer in three of those contests.

After returning briefly to the United States, the squad traveled to China for an eight-game tournament against top teams from other countries. The United States went 8–0 to win the tournament, while Cuba and China tied for second with 4–4 records.

In March 1996, during a short break in the national team's training schedule, Ruthie joined her family in a recording studio. For years the Boltons had enjoyed singing gospel songs together. Finally, the family decided to make a compact disc. Ruthie and 74 of her brothers, sisters, nieces, and nephews recorded 17 songs. Three months later, 14 of those tunes were released on compact disc.

In May, Ruthie and her teammates flew to Australia, and ran their record to 42–0 by winning all seven games they played in the Opals' World Challenge Tournament. They returned to North America and swept the Canadian national team in a three-game, three-city series in June. After some final tune-ups, the tournament Ruthie and her teammates had focused on for more than a year was at hand. It was finally time to play in the Olympics!

Once the Games began in Atlanta, Georgia, in late July, observers knew the year of intense training had paid off. The United States beat Cuba, 101–84, in the first matchup, then soundly defeated Ukraine and Zaire. With a victory over Australia, the United States headed into the medal round with a 4–0 record. Convincing victories over South Korea and Japan followed, sending the United States into another game against Australia in the semifinals. Again, the U.S. team won. Beating Brazil in the final game secured an 8–0 record in the Olympics and the gold medal.

Ruthie was on cloud nine for weeks following the Olympics. She enjoyed a brief vacation, then prepared to join a professional team in Turkey. Winning Olympic gold renewed Ruthie's enthusiasm for basketball. She was in excellent physical shape after more than a year with the national team.

Another reason influenced Ruthie's decision to play again in Europe. Two new professional women's leagues were forming in the United States: the American Basketball League (ABL) and the Women's National Basketball Association (WNBA). After initially agreeing to play in the ABL, Ruthie had finally decided to join the WNBA. Playing another season in Europe would help Ruthie stay sharp until WNBA play began in June 1997.

Ruthie's winning ways followed her to Europe. Her team finished first in the league, and Ruthie finished her final pro season in Europe with a championship.

Ruthie takes a break from her pregame stretching.

After traveling overseas for six years, Ruthie was finally getting a chance to pursue a career in her own country. She would join the Sacramento Monarchs in California. "I'm looking forward to it," Ruthie said before the initial WNBA season began.

Ruthie got off to a great start with the Monarchs. She was named the WNBA's very first player of the week after averaging 21.5 points, 8.5 rebounds, and 3.5 assists in the first three games. By season's end, she had led the 10–18 Monarchs in scoring 17 times and rebounding seven times. She hit 66 three-pointers to rank second in the league. Her 19.4 points per game was also second in the league.

Off the court, Ruthie made a difference with kids. She served as the 1998 national spokeswoman for the WNBA's youth health and fitness campaign. She toured 18 cities during the offseason, speaking to kids about staying fit. She was especially active in Sacramento, working with kids, raising money for a teen center, and hosting basketball clinics. The Sacramento YWCA gave Ruthie its Touching Lives Award for her contributions to the community.

Ruthie also continues to compete for USA Basketball programs. She played in the Women's International Invitational Tournament held in September 1997. Then she was a member of the U.S. team that won a gold medal in the 1998 World Championships at Germany.

Through the WNBA, Ruthie is making the most of her chance to pursue a pro basketball career in the United States.

At the same time, Ruthie is making plans for her future. She plans to get a license to practice massage therapy when she retires from playing and is considering coaching basketball part time. She also wants to work with at-risk teens—that is, teenagers who are engaging in or might be tempted to try activities that could harm their future, such as abusing alcohol or drugs. "After I finish my basketball career, I want to become a counselor for teenagers," she said. "I think I have a lot to share with young people."

Mae Ola, who has taught at-risk teenagers at a high school in Lake City, Florida, agrees. "I brought Ruthie to school to talk to the students, and I saw them undergo an instant attitude change," she said. "I've never seen the kids respond so positively to anyone before."

Ruthie leads kids through fitness drills. She conducted many clinics throughout the country.

When talking to youngsters, Ruthie emphasizes the importance of having a positive attitude. A lot of kids think they can make it in pro sports if they're physically gifted, she notes, but it takes more than that. You have to work hard, have a good attitude, and believe in yourself, she says. "No matter how good you are at something, you can be even greater if you believe in yourself," Ruthie said. "You can't control what other people say or do, but you can control your attitude."

Ruthie also encourages youngsters not to be discouraged by people who don't believe they can achieve their dreams. "If their expectations for you are negative, make them positive," she said. "I've had to exceed other people's expectations throughout my whole career."

With a positive attitude like that, it's no wonder Ruthie Bolton-Holifield has achieved her dreams.

Career Highlights

Auburn University Lady Tigers

Season	Games	Field Goals			Free Throws			Points	Points per Game	Rebounds	Rebounds per Game
		Made	Attempted	%	Made	Attempted	%				
1985-86	30	137	257	.533	22	35	.629	296	9.9	143	4.8
1986-87	33	125	240	.521	25	34	735	275	8.3	96	2.9
1987-88	35	145	265	.547	40	54	.741	335	9.6	108	3.1
1988-89	34	123	276	.446	21	34	.618	270	7.9	143	4.2
Totals	132	530	1,038	.511	108	157	.688	1,176	8.9	490	3.7

Olympics

Year	Games	Field Goals			Free Throws			Points	Points per Game	Rebounds	Rebounds per Game
		Made	Attempted	%	Made	Attempted	%				
1996	8	36	81	.444	15	21	.714	102	12.8	34	4.3

Sacramento Monarchs

Season	Games	Field Goals			Free Throws			Points	Points per Game	Rebounds	Rebounds per Game
		Made	Attempted	%	Made	Attempted	%				
1997	23	164	408	.402	53	69	.768	447	19.4	133	5.8
1998	5	17	58	.293	17	28	.607	55	11.0	11	2.2
Totals	28	181	466	.388	70	97	.722	502	17.9	144	5.1

Career Honors

- All-WNBA first team, 1997.
- Gold medal winner, World Championships, 1998.
- Gold medal winner, Goodwill Games, 1994, 1998.
- Gold medal winner, Olympics, 1996.
- Bronze medal winner, World Championships, 1994.
- USA Basketball Female Player of the Year, 1991.
- All-SEC second team, 1989.
- NCAA Mideast Region All-Tournament Team, 1988, 1989.
- SEC All-Academic Team, 1988, 1989.
- NCAA Final Four All-Tournament Team, 1988.

Glossary

assists: Passes that lead directly to points.

exhibition games: Matchups played under usual game conditions, but which do not count in any official way.

free-throw lane: The area, usually 12 feet wide, under each basket extending from the baseline to the free-throw line.

inbounded: Having passed the ball into play from out of bounds.

key: An area of the court made up of the free-throw lane and the free-throw circle.

layup: A shot in which the shooter dribbles toward the basket, jumps off one foot, then gently bounces the ball off the backboard and into the net.

point guard: The player who is responsible for running a team's offense by dribbling and passing the ball to teammates.

rebound: The act of gaining possession of the ball after a missed shot.

scholarship: A grant of money given to a student to help pay education costs.

three-point range: The distance from the basket, marked by a line, behind which a made shot is worth three points. In international competition, the line is placed 20 feet, 6.1 inches from the basket. In college and professional women's leagues, it's 19 feet, 9 inches.

tip-off: The start of a basketball game.

Ruthie and Mae Ola

Sources

Information for this book was obtained from the following sources: Auburn Media Relations; Debbie Becker (*USA Today*, 25 May 1995, 10 January 1996); *The Birmingham News*, 3 January 1996, 4 January 1996, 4 April 1996, 17 June 1996, 5 August 1996; *Birmingham Post-Herald*, 4 January 1996, 15 July 1996; the author's interview with Mae Ola Bolton, 22 May 1997; the author's interviews with Ruthie Bolton-Holifield, 28 January 1997, 30 January 1997, 10 April 1997; *The Denver Post*, 5 August 1996; Oscar Dixon (*USA Today*, 10 January 1996); Dennis Dube (*The Auburn Plainsman*, 11 January 1996); *Ebony*, March 1996; Mark Murphy (*Inside the Auburn Tigers*, January 1995); *Mobile Press Register*, 21 April 1996; *Montgomery Advertiser*, 7 July 1996, 22 July 1996; *The New York Times*, 5 August 1996; *Opelika-Auburn News*, 31 December 1995, 20 June 1996, 29 July 1996, 30 July 1996; Chuck Schoffner (The Associated Press, 21 April 1996); Miki Turner (*Essence*, April 1996); USA Basketball news releases; USA Basketball tour reviews; The 1996 USA Women's Olympic Basketball Team Media Guide; and Steve Wieberg (*USA Today*, 26 July 1996, 5 August 1996).

Index

Write to Ruthie

You can send mail to Ruthie at the address on the right. If you write a letter, don't get your hopes up too high. Ruthie and other athletes get lots of letters every day, and they aren't always able to answer them all.

Ruthie Bolton-Holifield
c/o Sacramento Monarchs
1 Sports Pkwy
Sacramento CA 95834

Acknowledgments

Photographs are reproduced by permission of: Andrew D. Bernstein/NBA Photos, pp. 1, 10; Steven Freeman/NBA Photos, pp. 2, 9; Nathaniel S. Butler/NBA Photos, p. 6; © ALLSPORT USA/Doug Pensinger, p. 8; Scott Cunningham/NBA Photos, p. 13; Ruthie Bolton Foundation, pp. 14, 16, 19, 35, 46, 61; © ALLSPORT USA/David Klutho, pp. 22, 24; © Barry Fikes/courtesy Auburn Athletic Department, pp. 25, 28, 29; SportsChrome East/West, Rich Kane, pp. 32, 50; Lou Capozzola/NBA Photos, p. 38; © ALLSPORT USA, p. 40; © ALLSPORT USA/Chris Cole, p. 44; Rocky Widner/NBA Photos, p. 48, 58; © Rod Searcey, p. 52; Norm Perdue/NBA Photos, p. 55; and © ALLSPORT USA/Todd Warshaw, p. 57. Front cover photograph reproduced by permission of © ALLSPORT USA/Craig Jones. Back cover photograph reproduced by permission of William R. Sallaz/NBA Photos.

About the Author

Terri Morgan is a freelance writer and sports fan who lives in Soquel, California. Her articles have appeared in over four dozen magazines and newspapers. Her other books for Lerner include *Photography: Take Your Best Shot, Chris Mullin: Sure Shot, Steve Young: Complete Quarterback* (all with Shmuel Thaler) and *Junior Seau: High Voltage Linebacker*. When not writing, Terri enjoys surfing, walking her dogs, playing baseball, and watching sports.